Adult Coloring Book

Folk Art Hand Drawn Designs

Paint for Fun

Roosters

Illustrations created by Esther Prentice

Copyright©2023 by Esther Prentice

Farm Fresh Hen

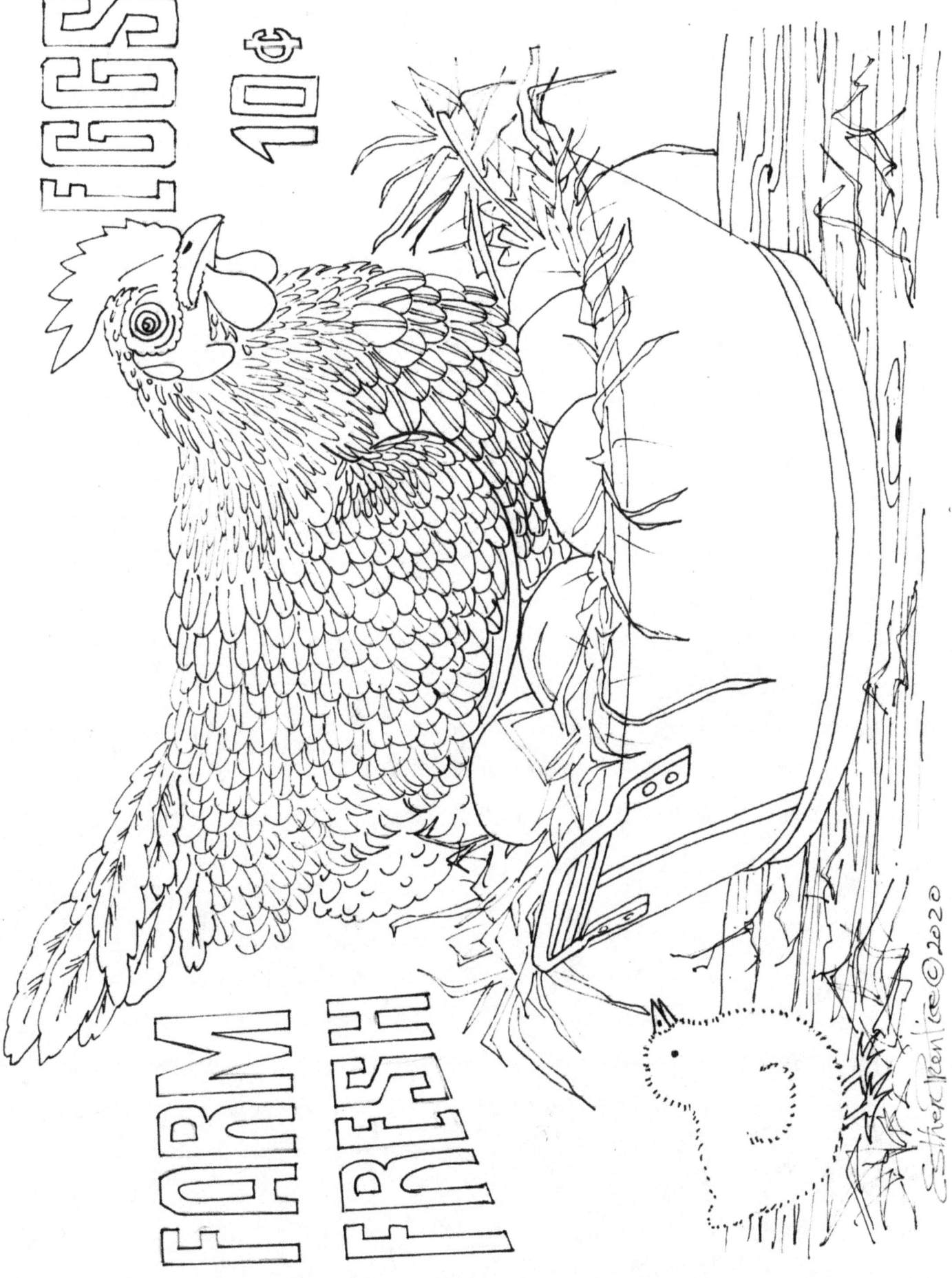

Folk Art Rooster 1

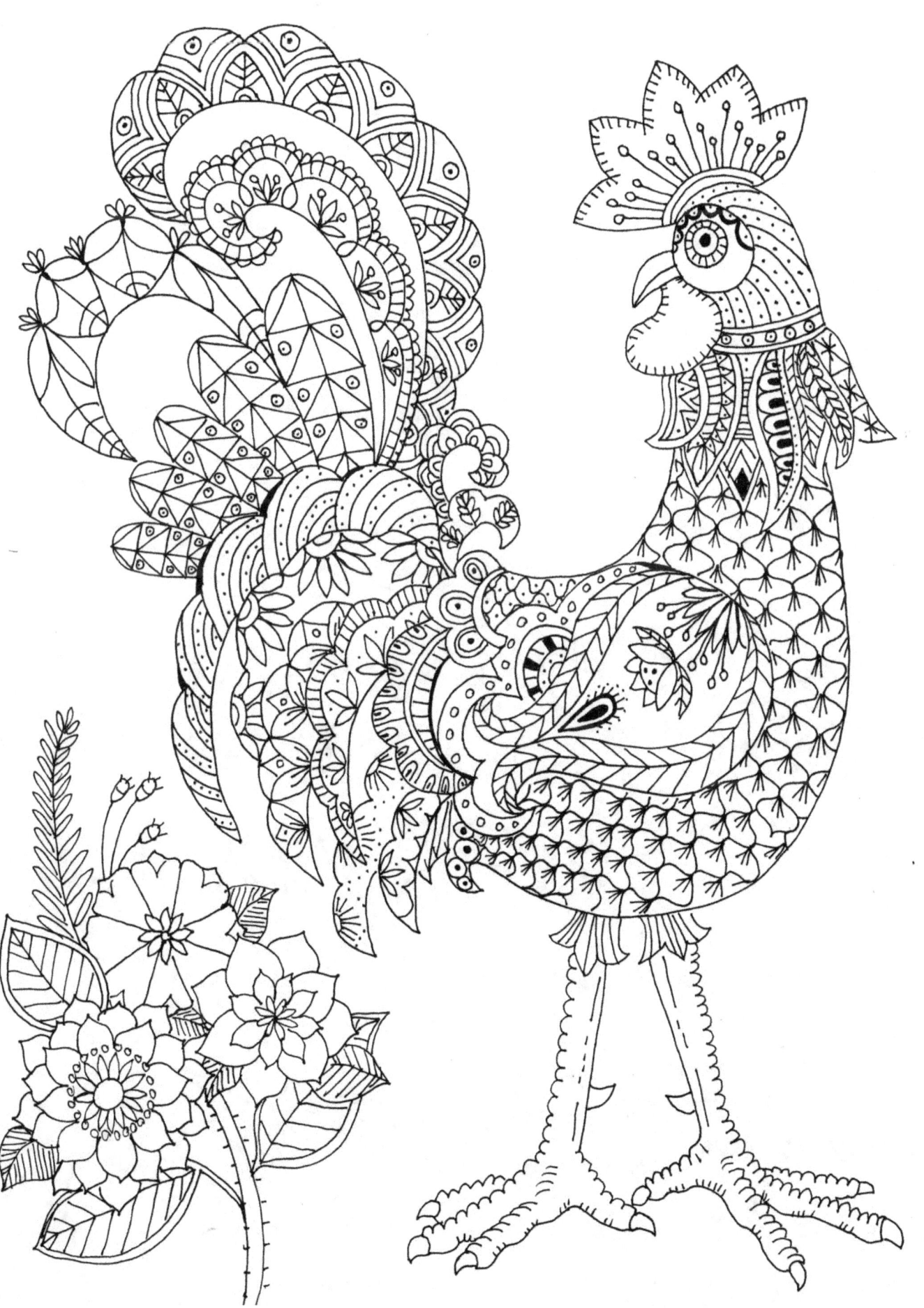

Cowboy Rooster

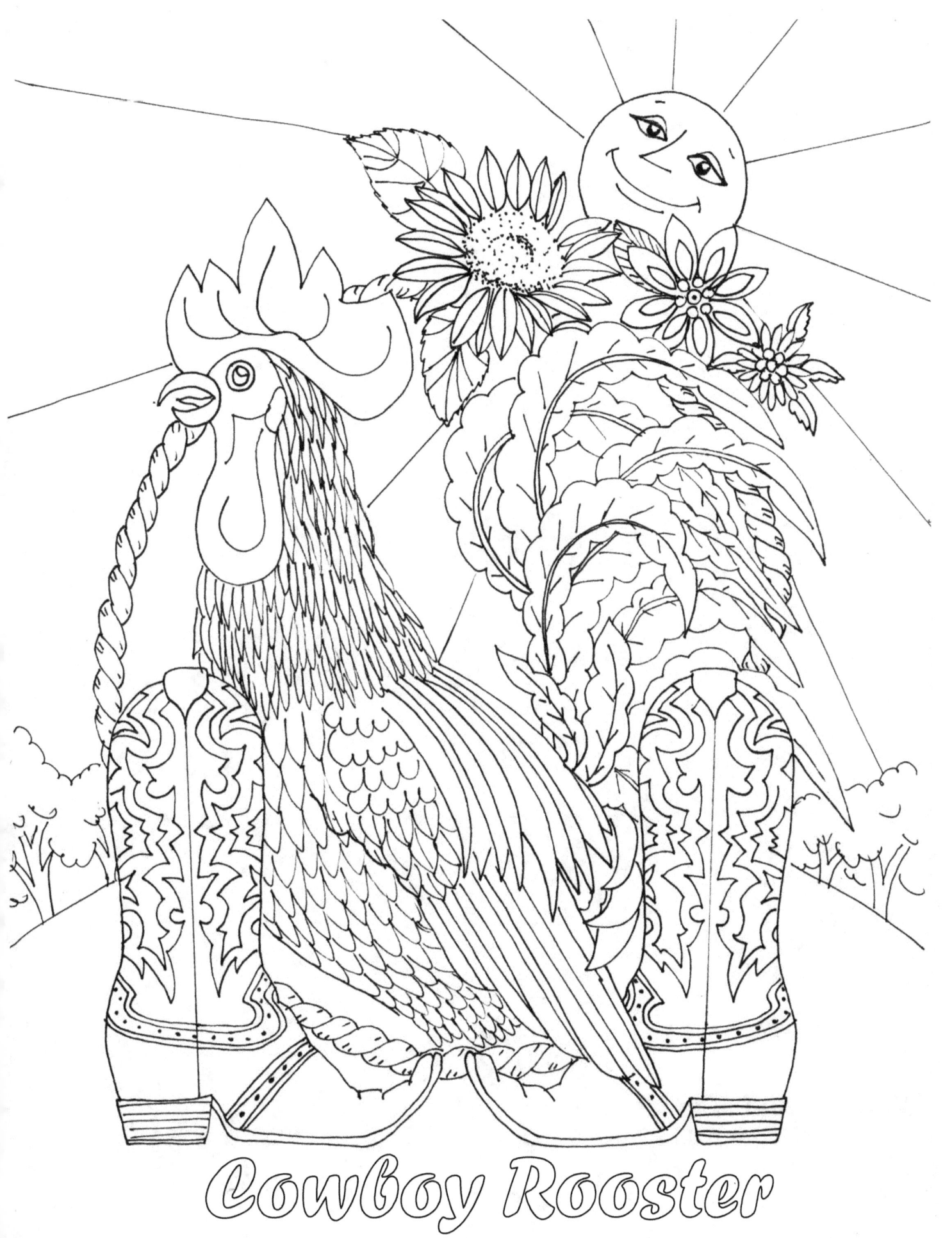

Cowboy Rooster

Rooster and Hen

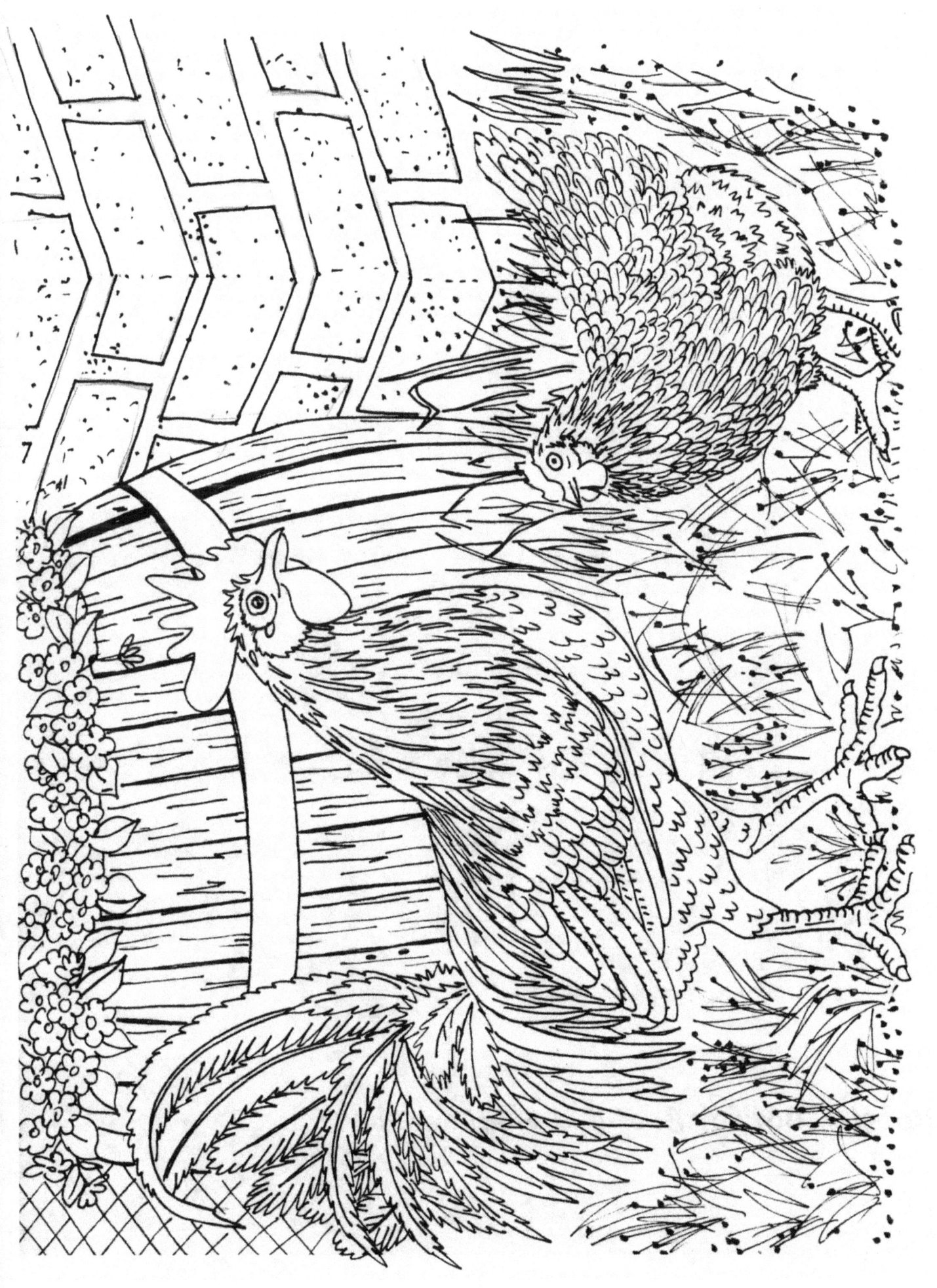

Rooster, Cowboy Boot and Sunflowers

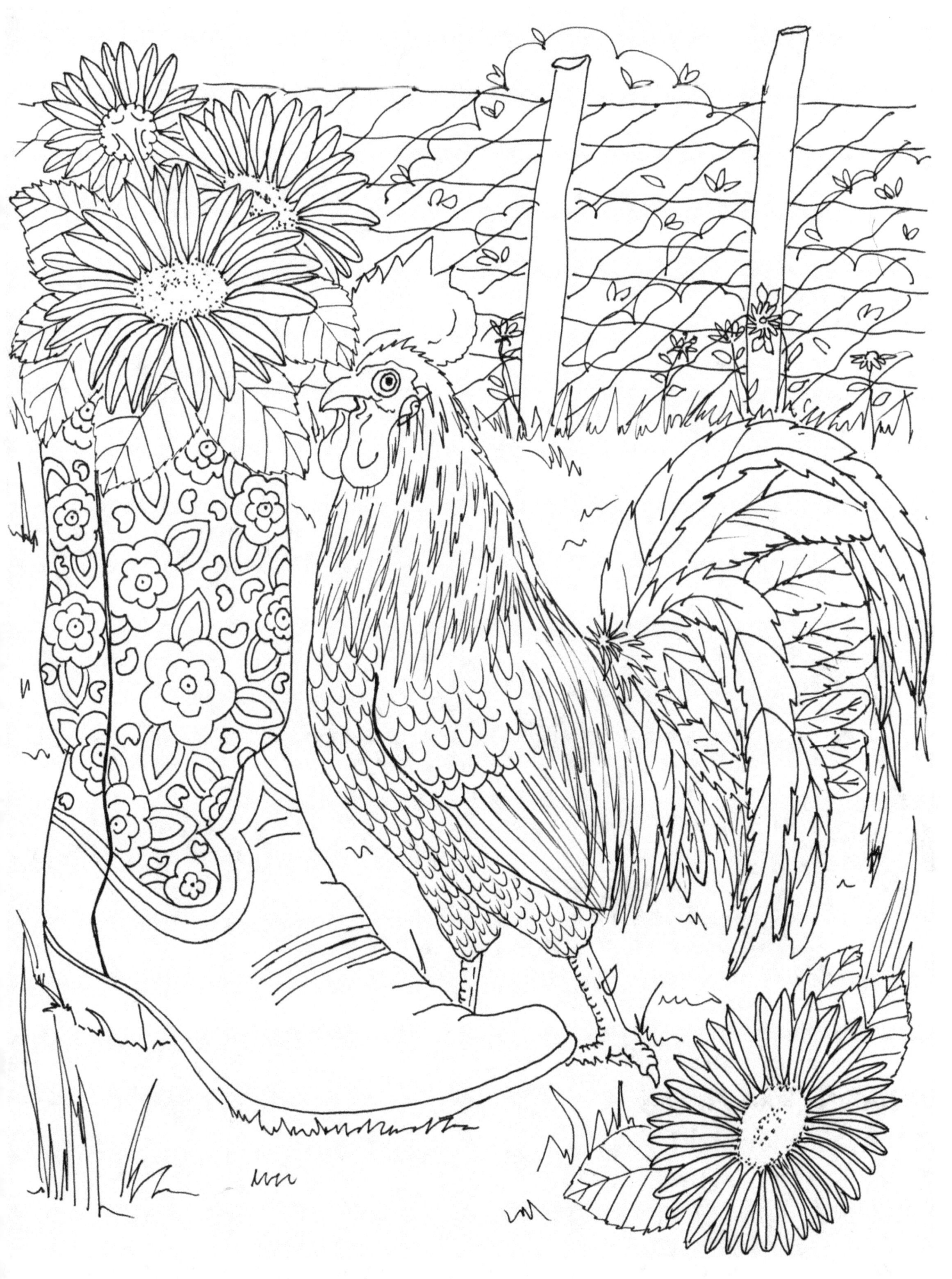

Rooster and Family

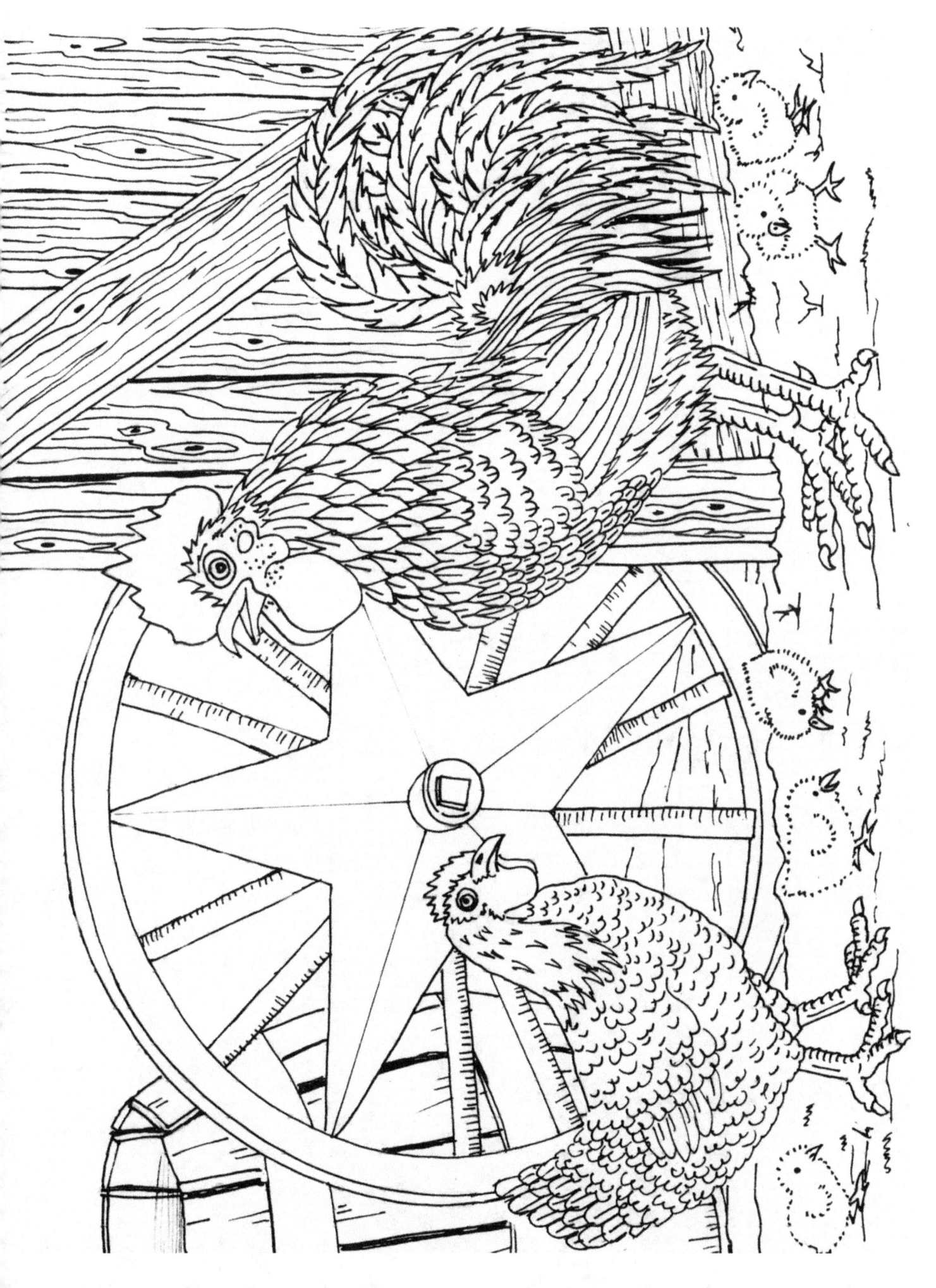

Welcome Rooster and Boot

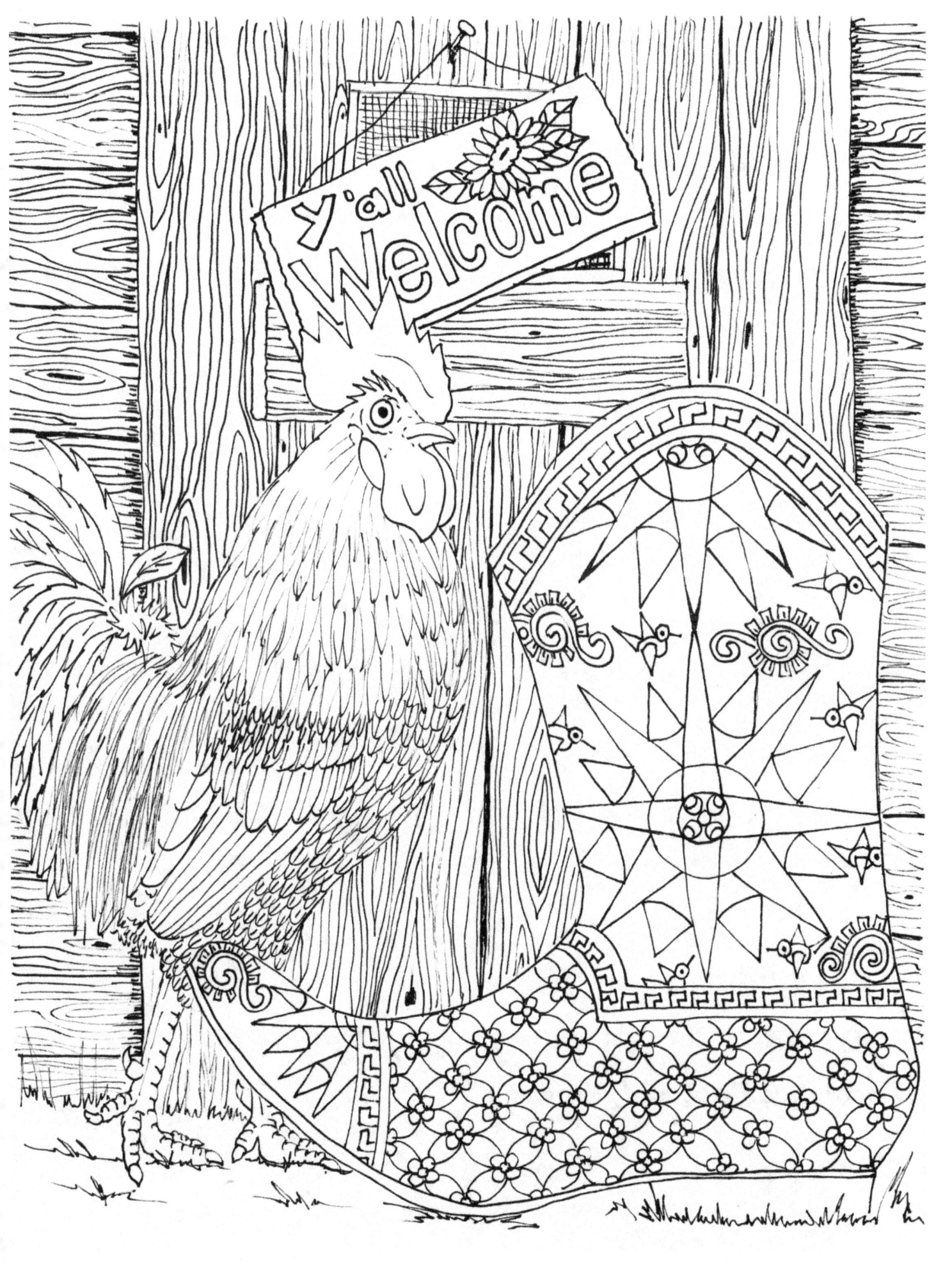

Decorative Boot and Rooster 1

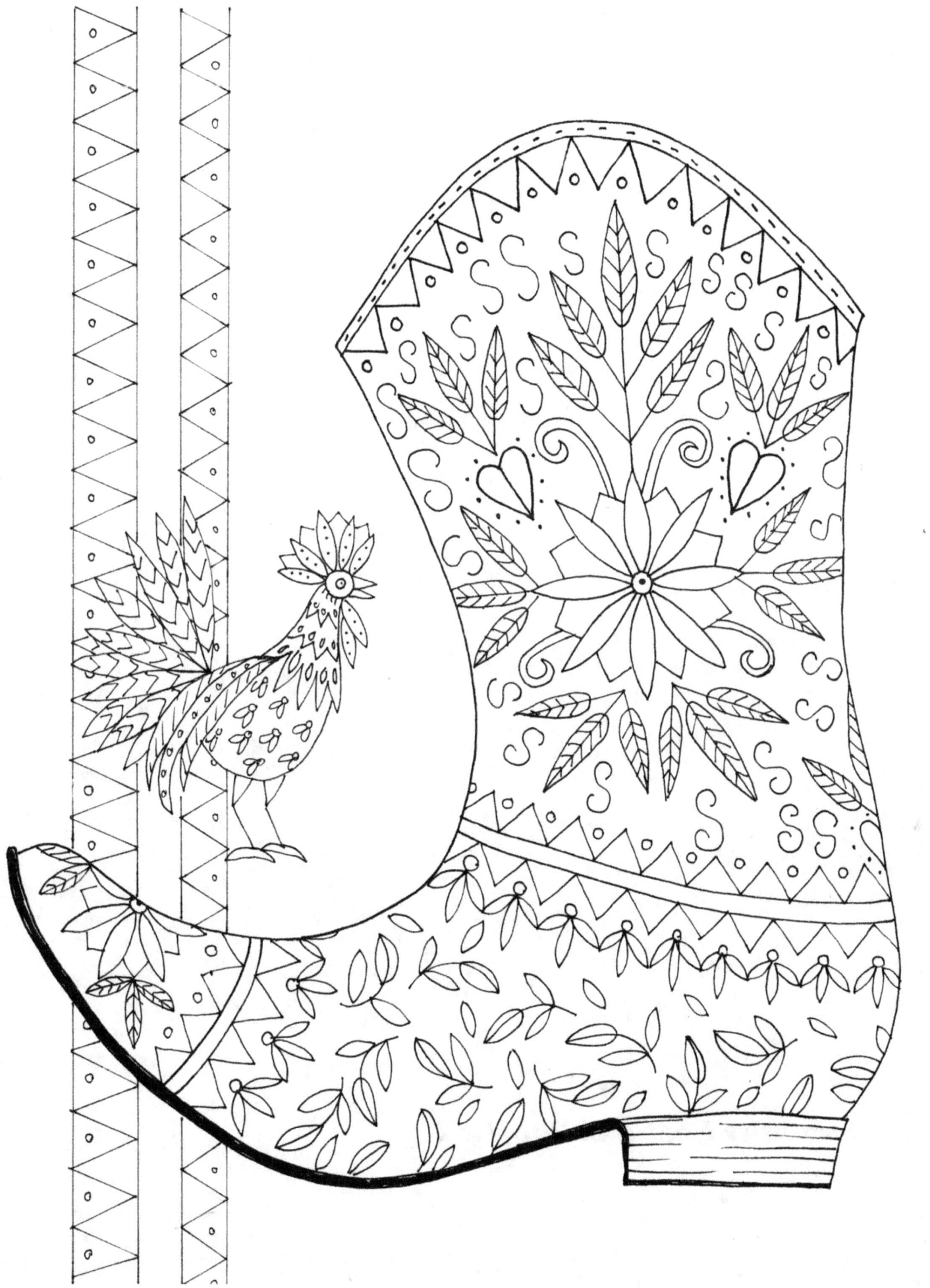

Decorative Boot and Rooster 2

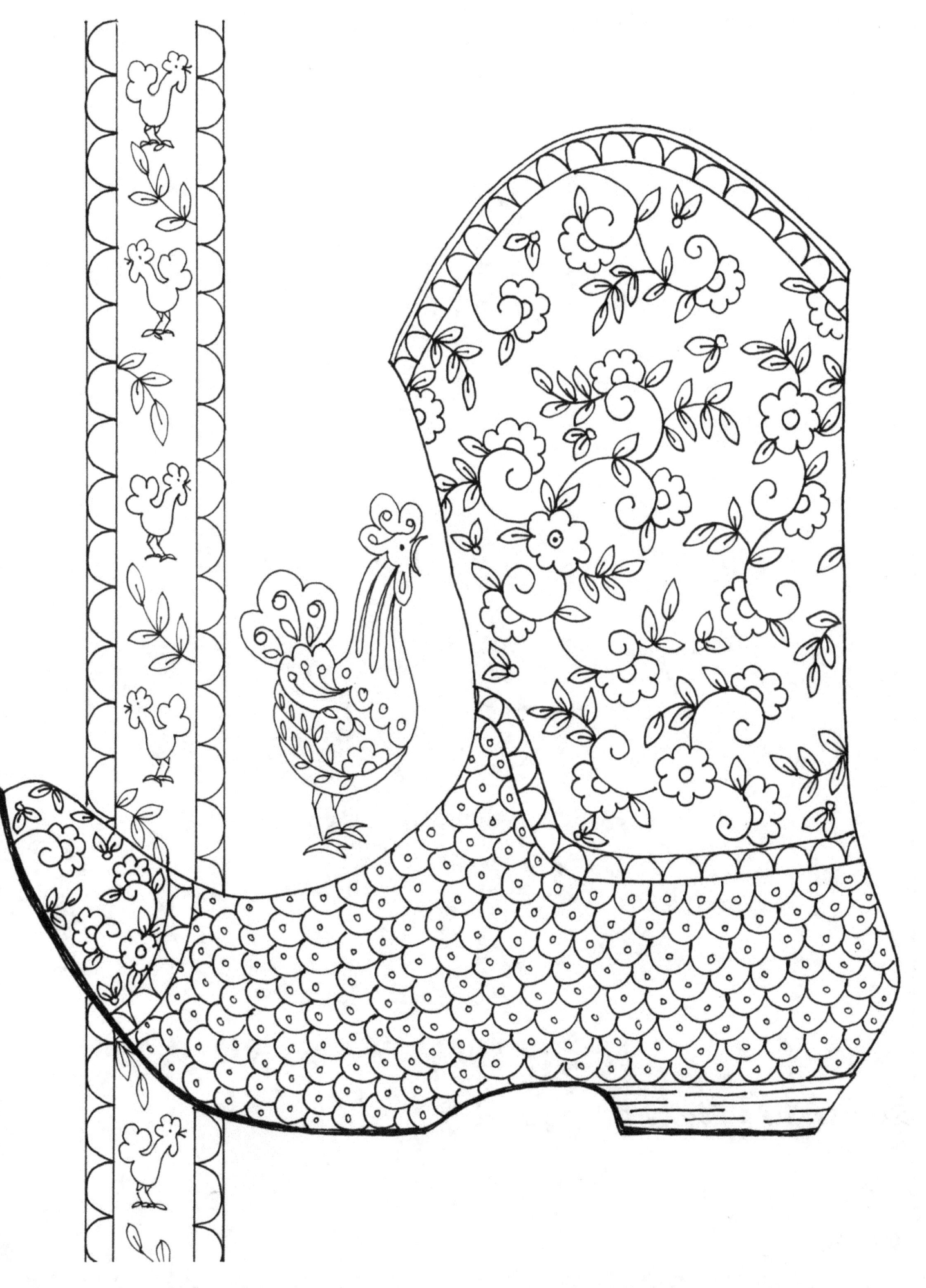

Rooster and Flowers

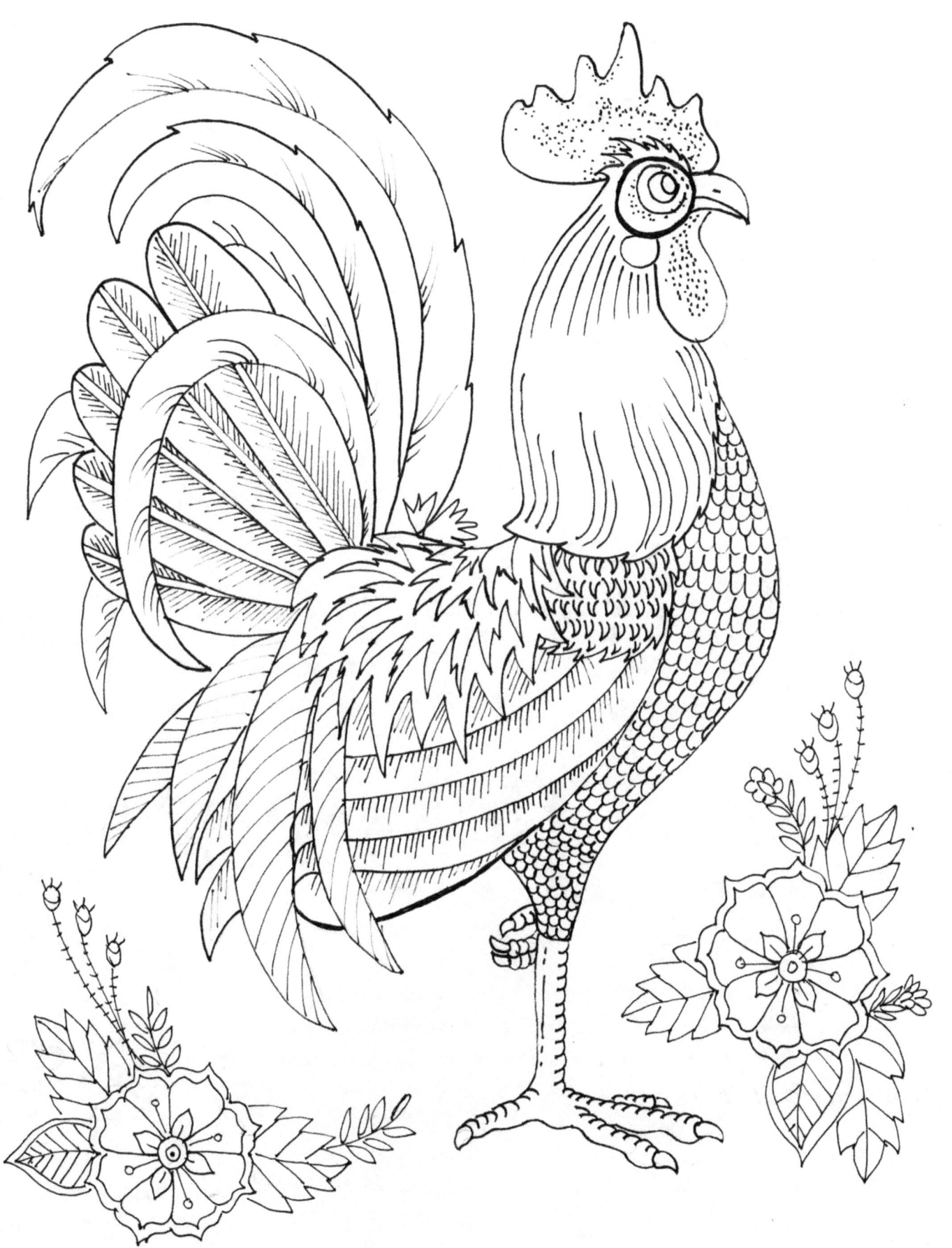

Americana Rooster

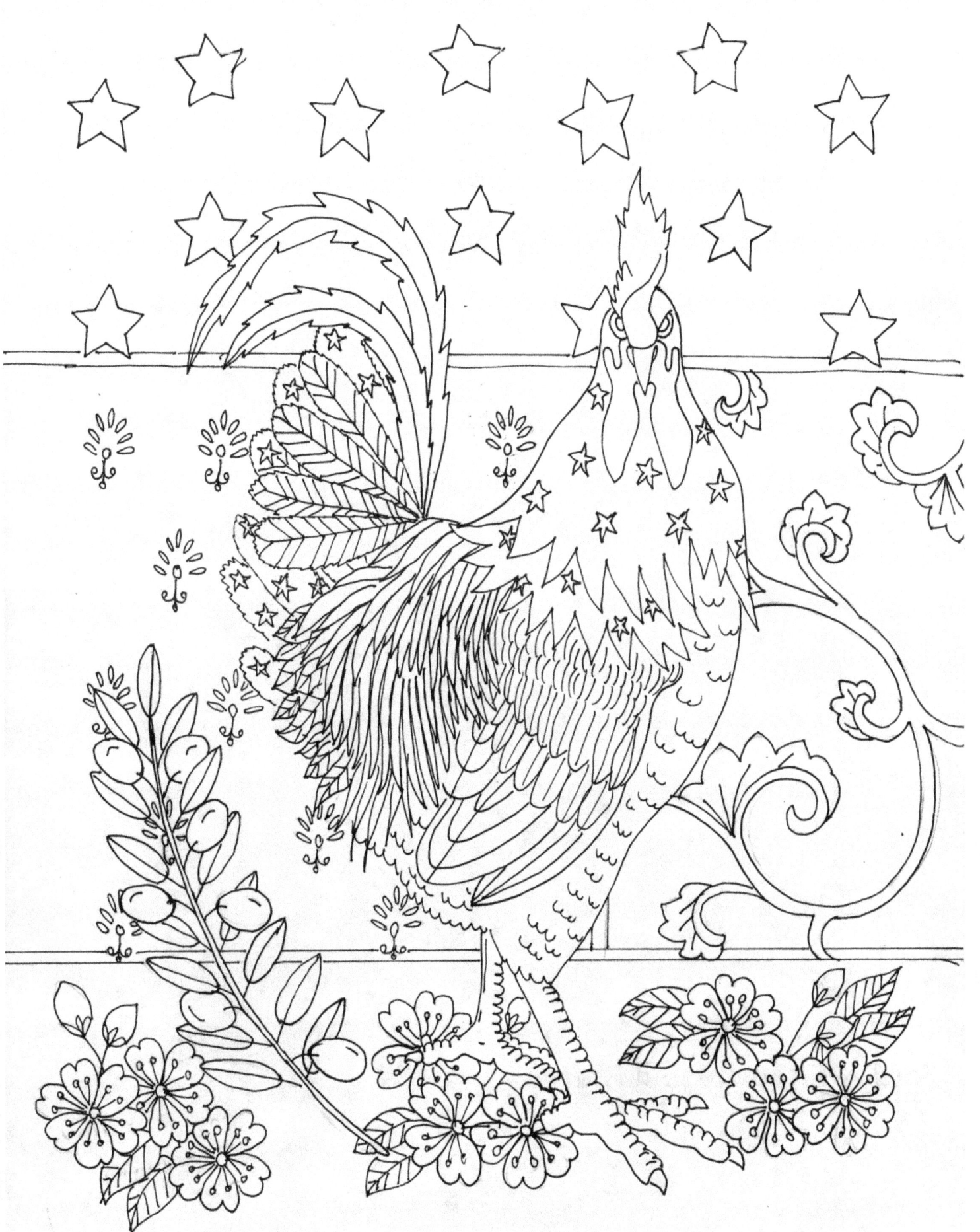

Folk Art Rooster and Fruit

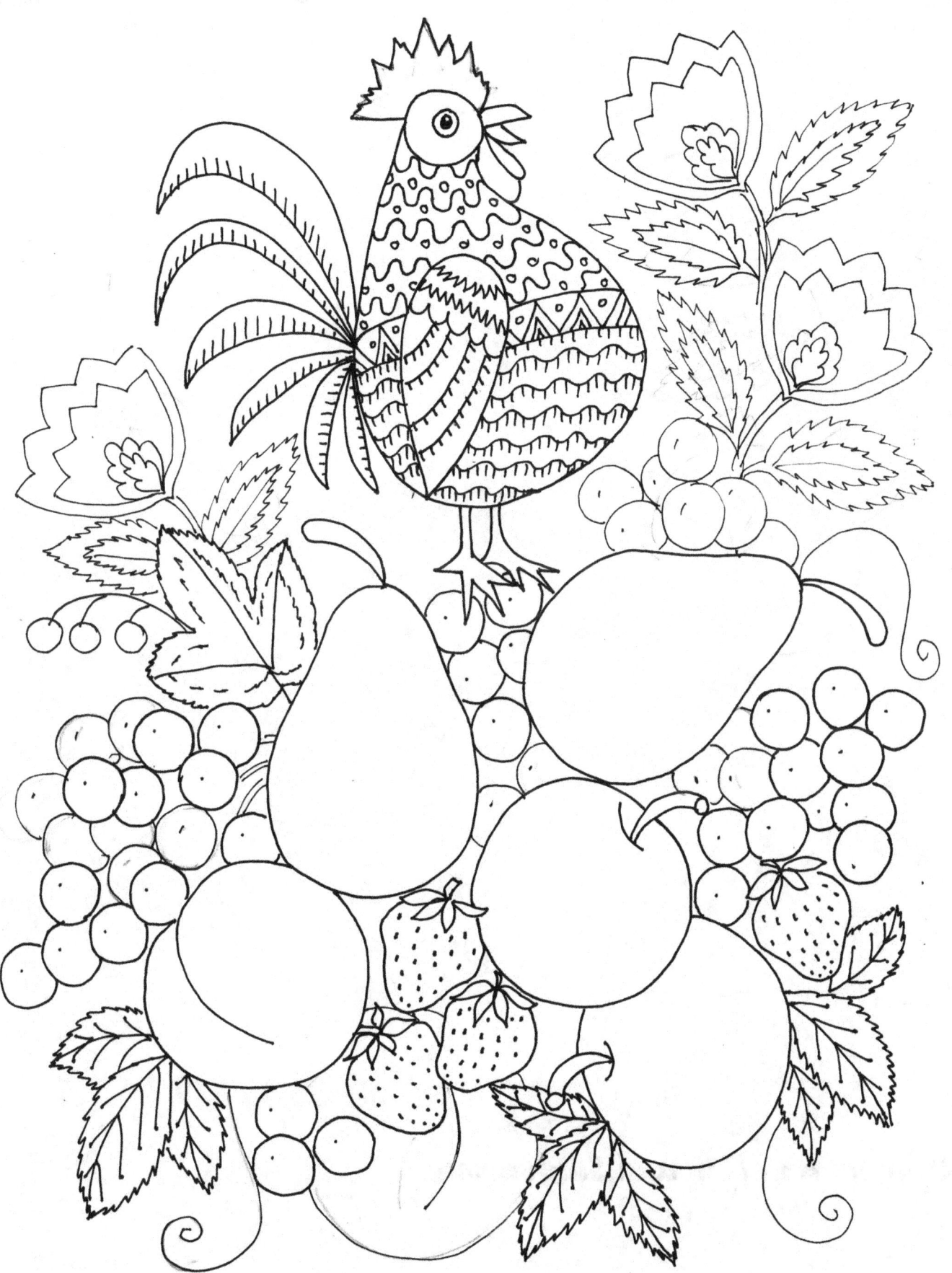

Rooster and Hen and Sunflowers

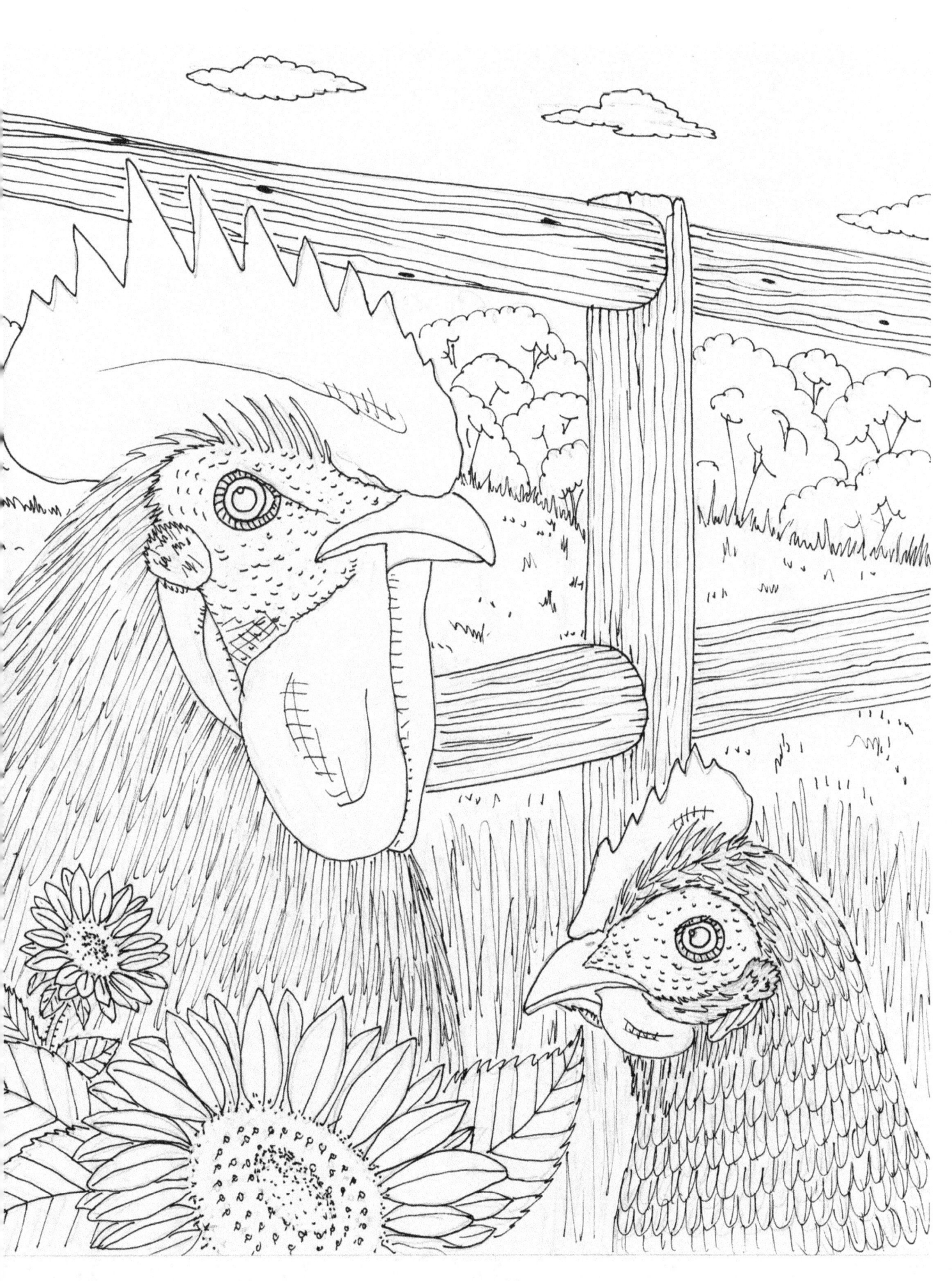

Majestic Rooster

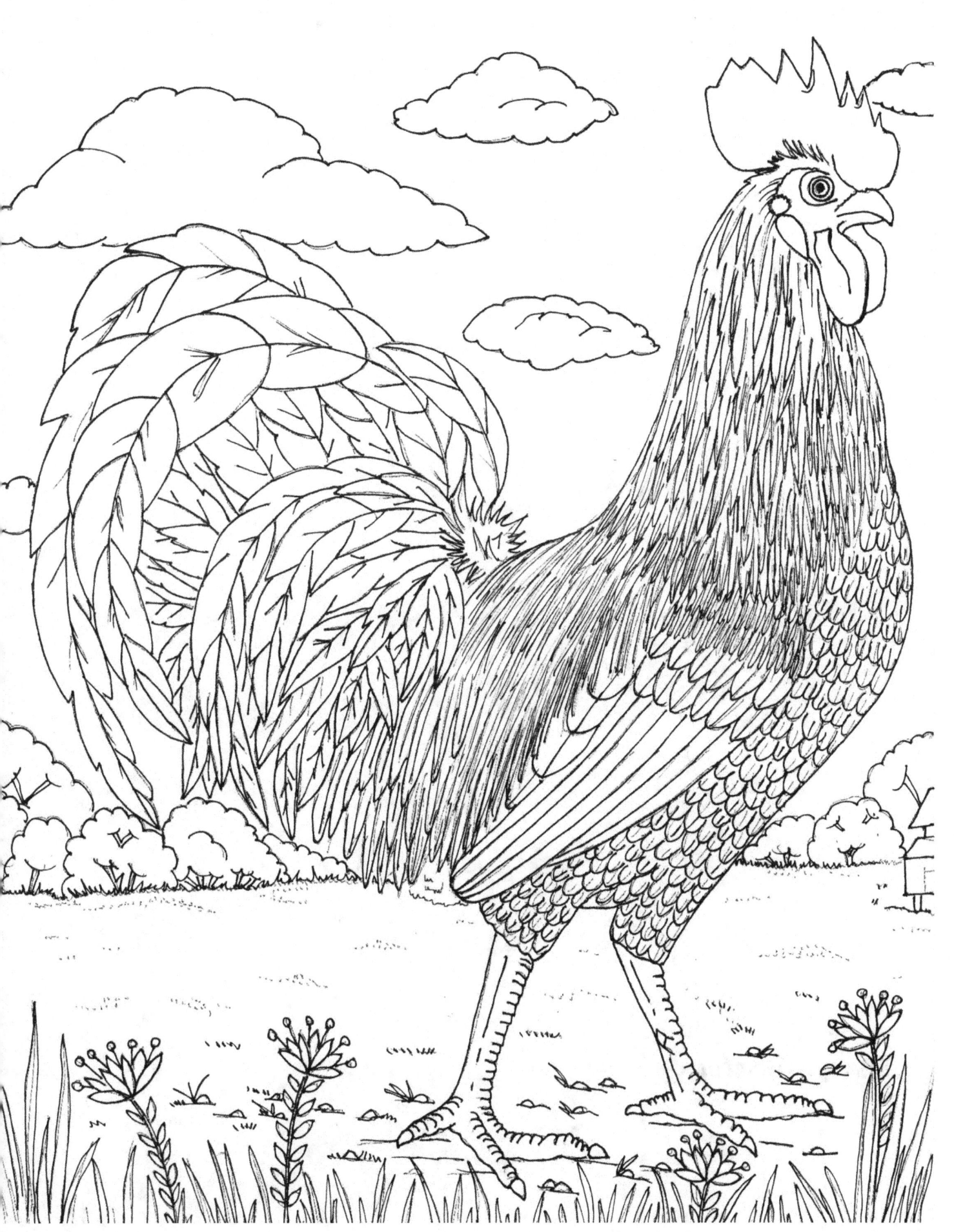

Fancy Rooster

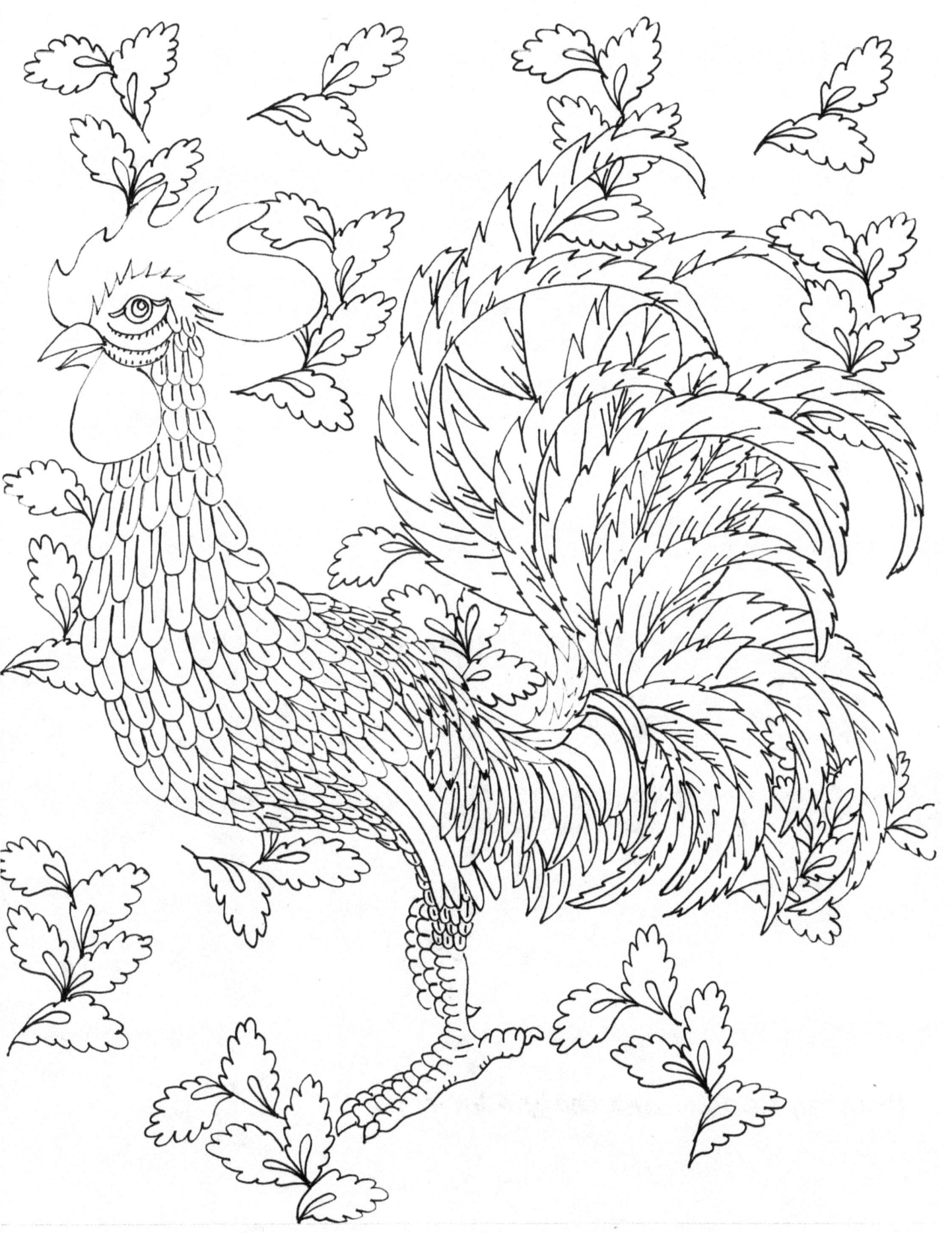

Crowing Rooster and Leafy Flowers

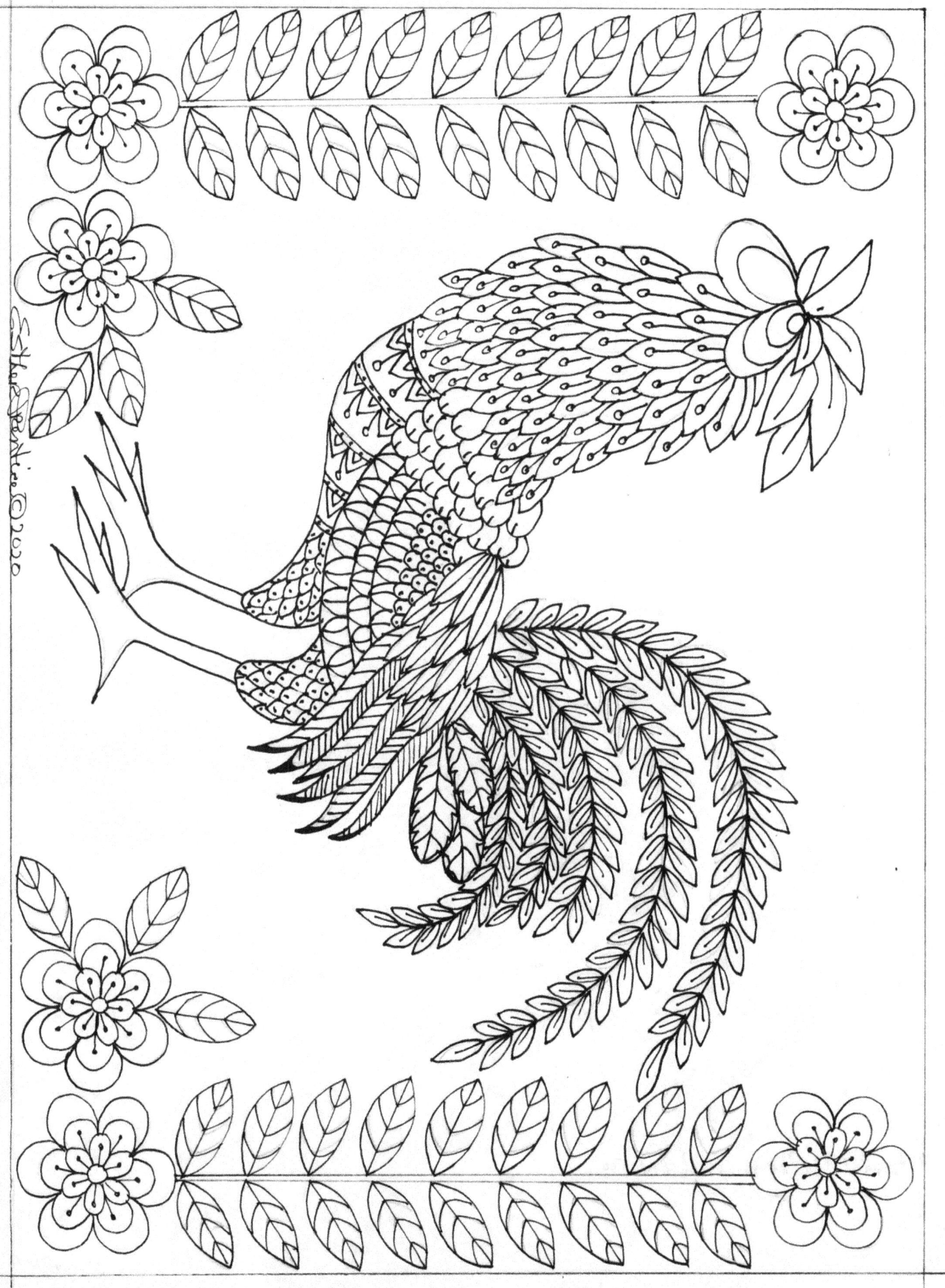

Trinity Tulips and Rooster

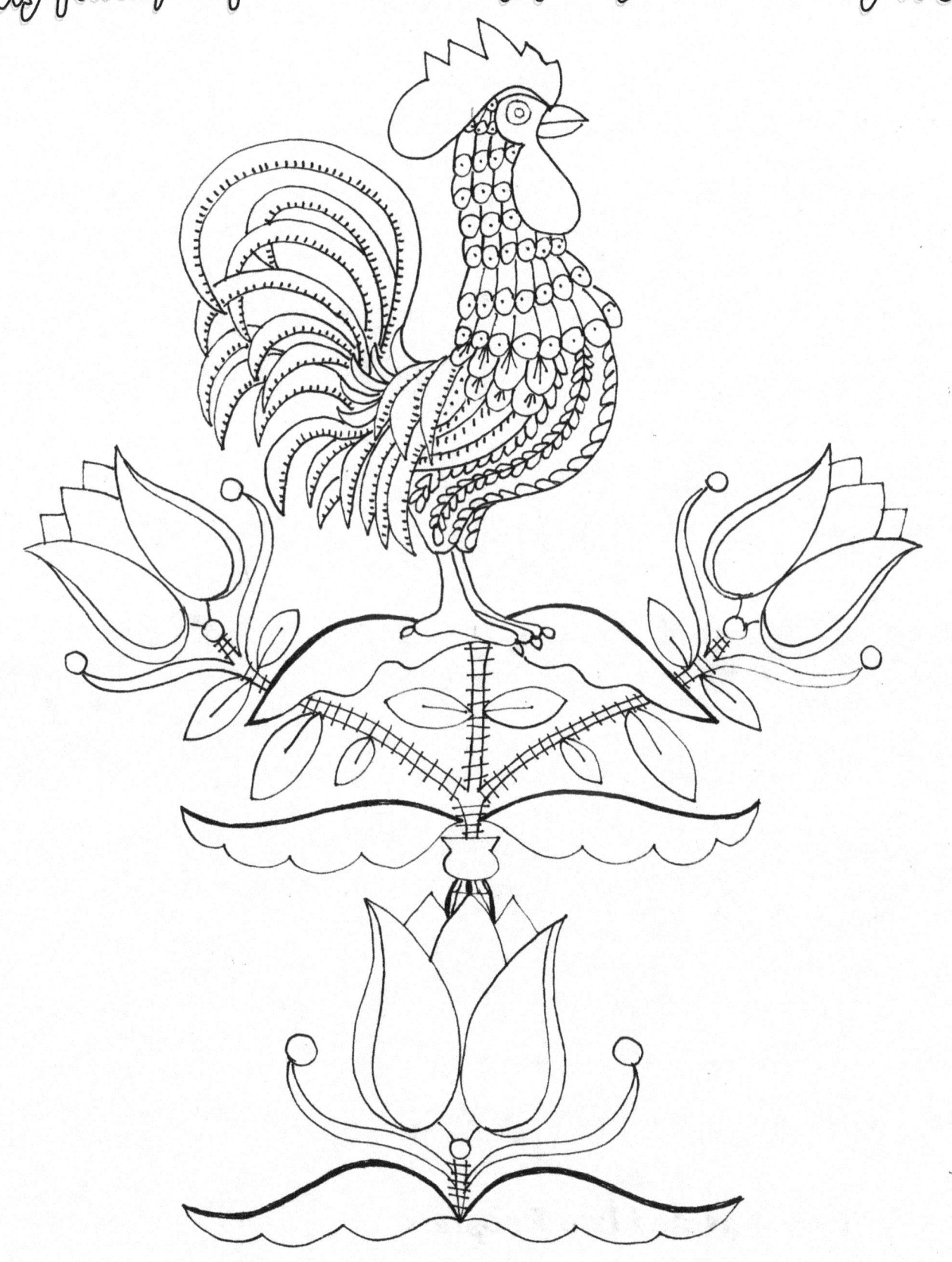

May faith, hope and charity fill your Country Home

Country Blessings and Two Roosters

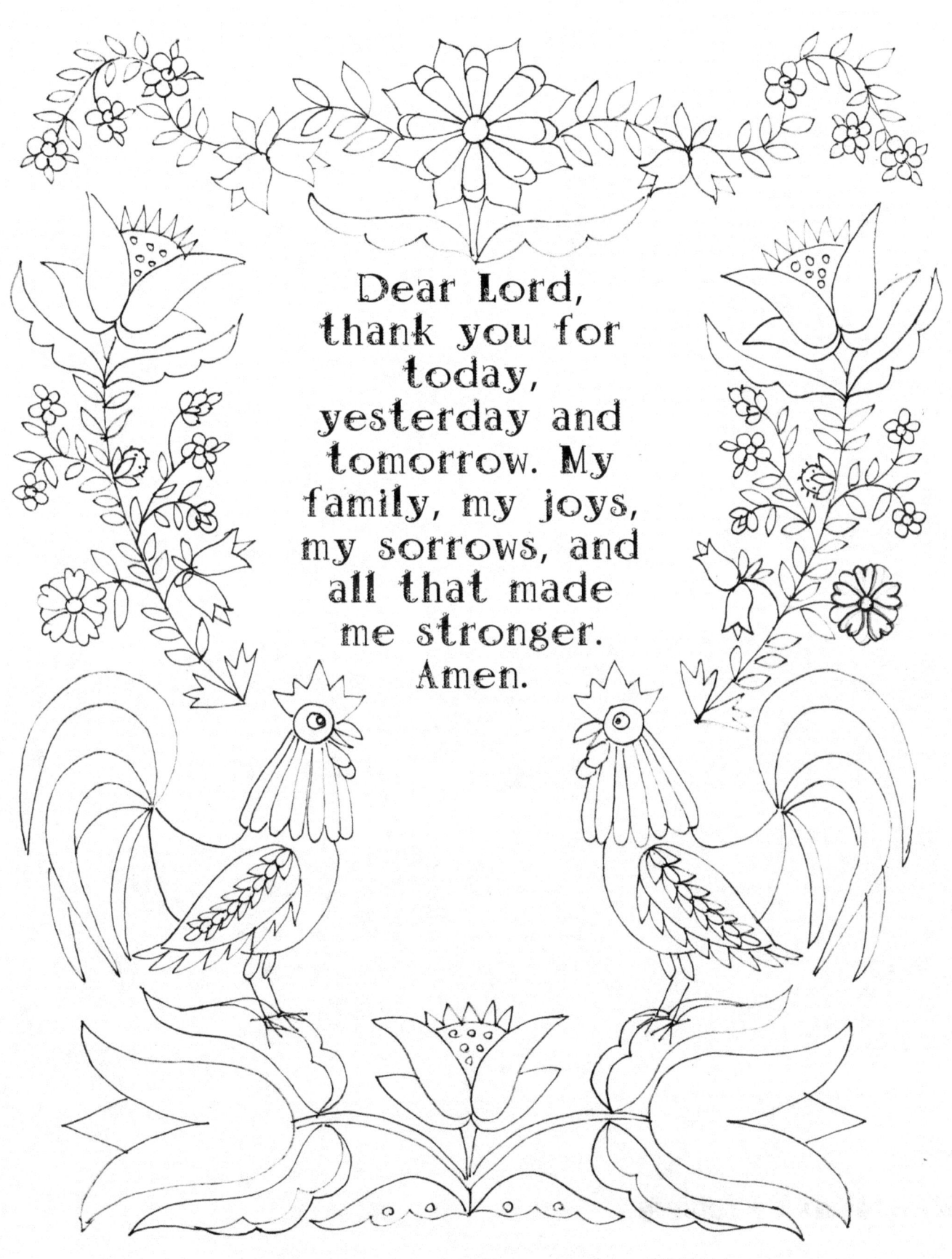

Dear Lord,
thank you for
today,
yesterday and
tomorrow. My
family, my joys,
my sorrows, and
all that made
me stronger.
Amen.

Country Blessings

Rooster and Flowers

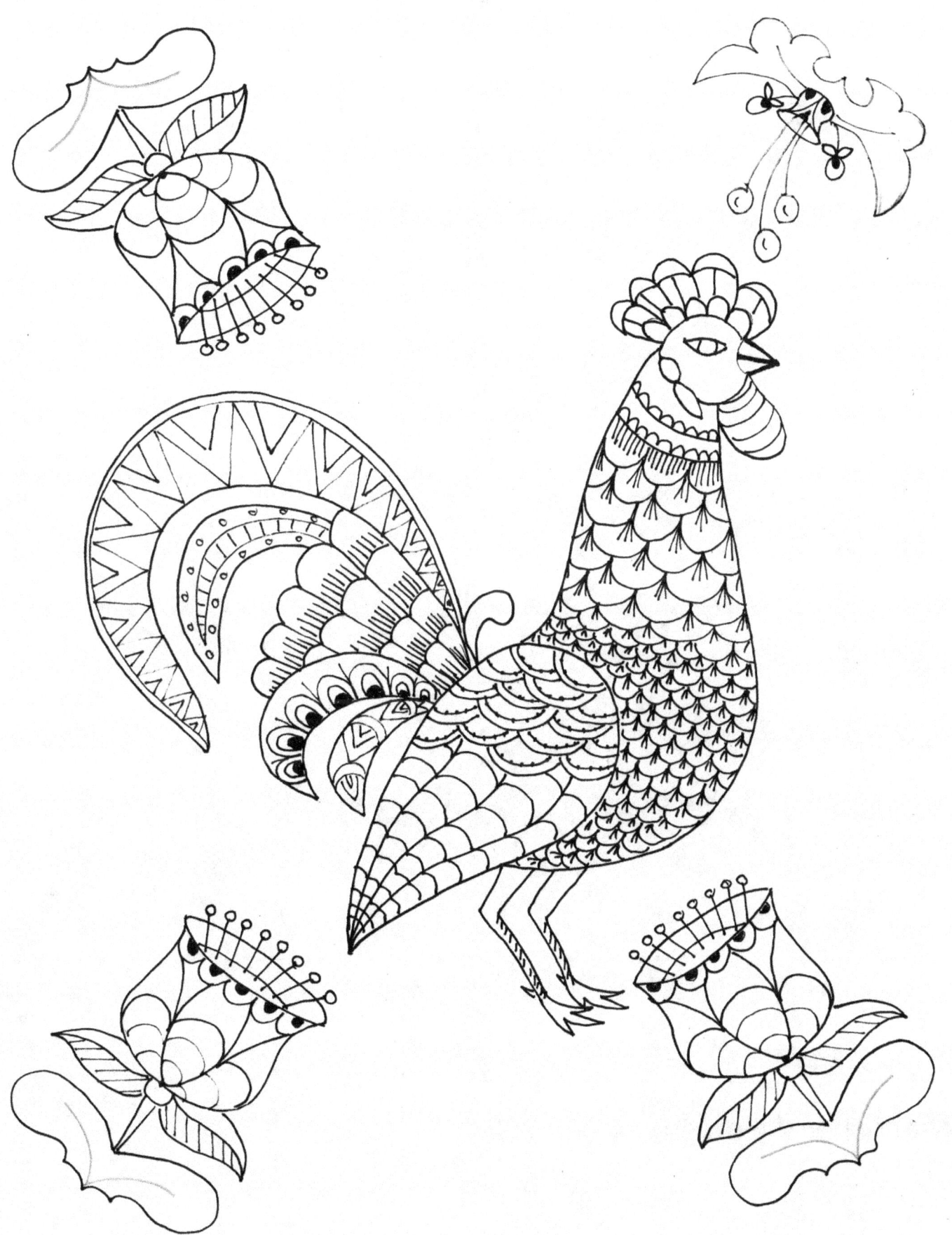

Rooster and Cactus

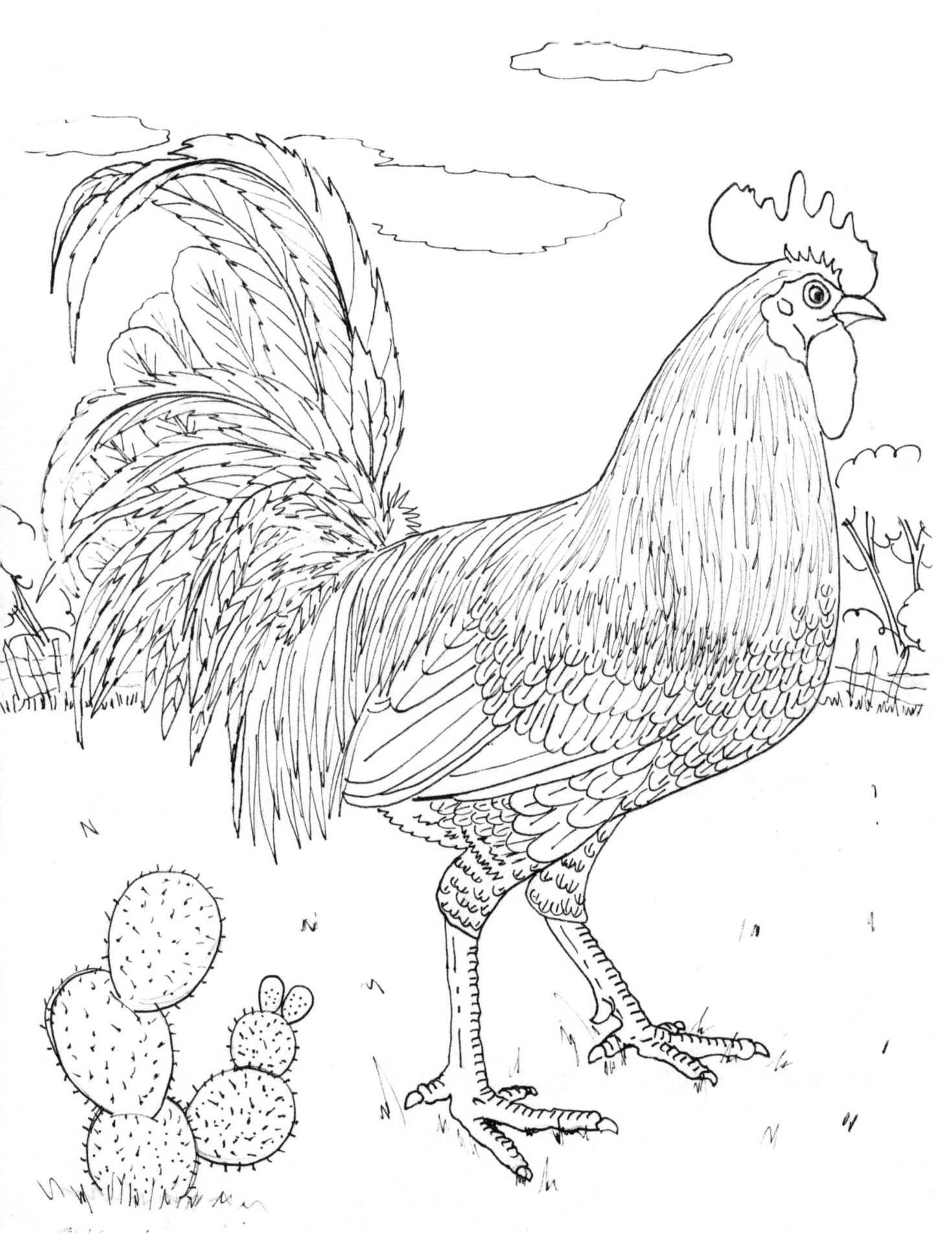

Barnyard Rooster and Cowboy Boots

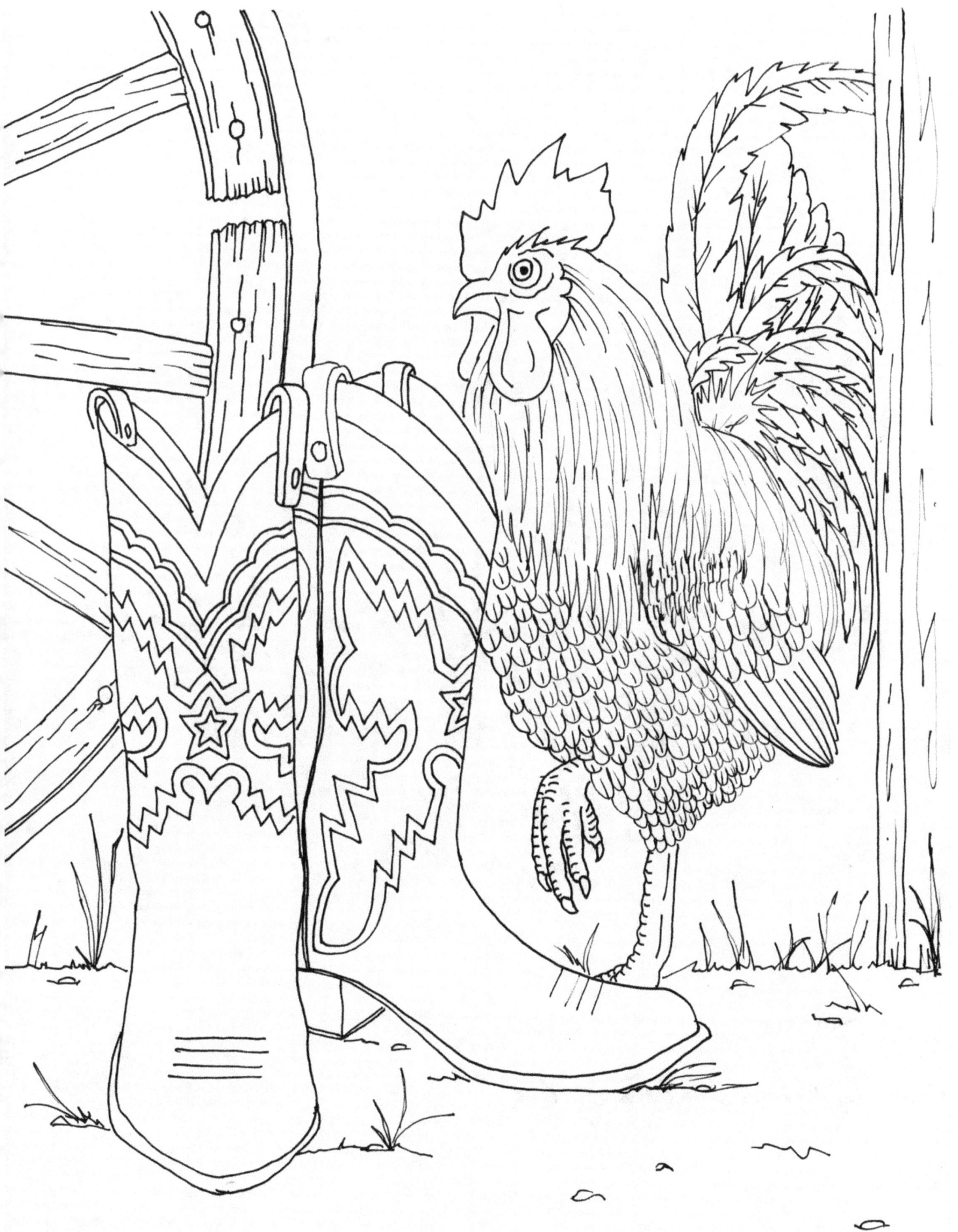

Decorative Rooster and Border

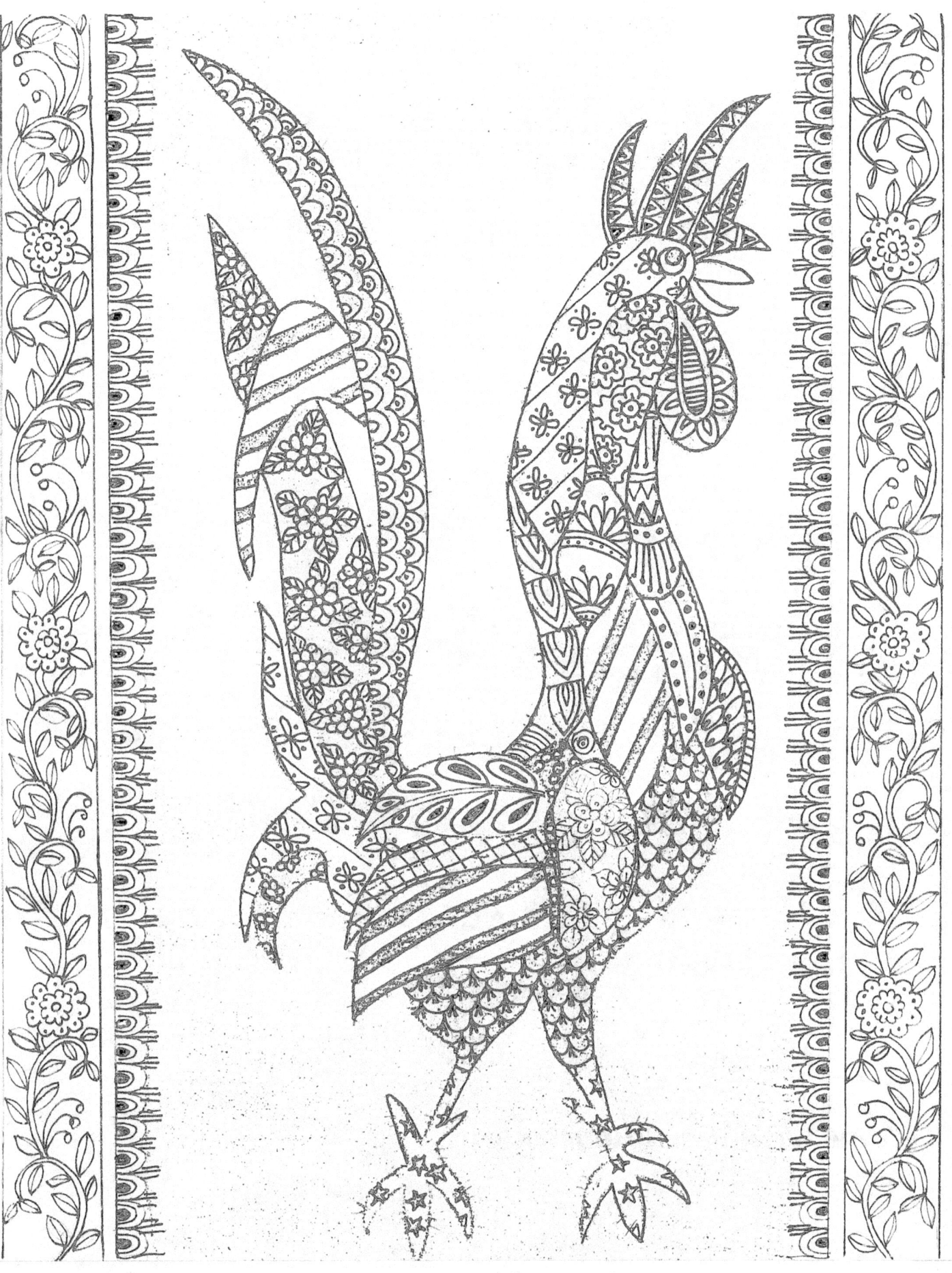

Floral Wreath and Rooster

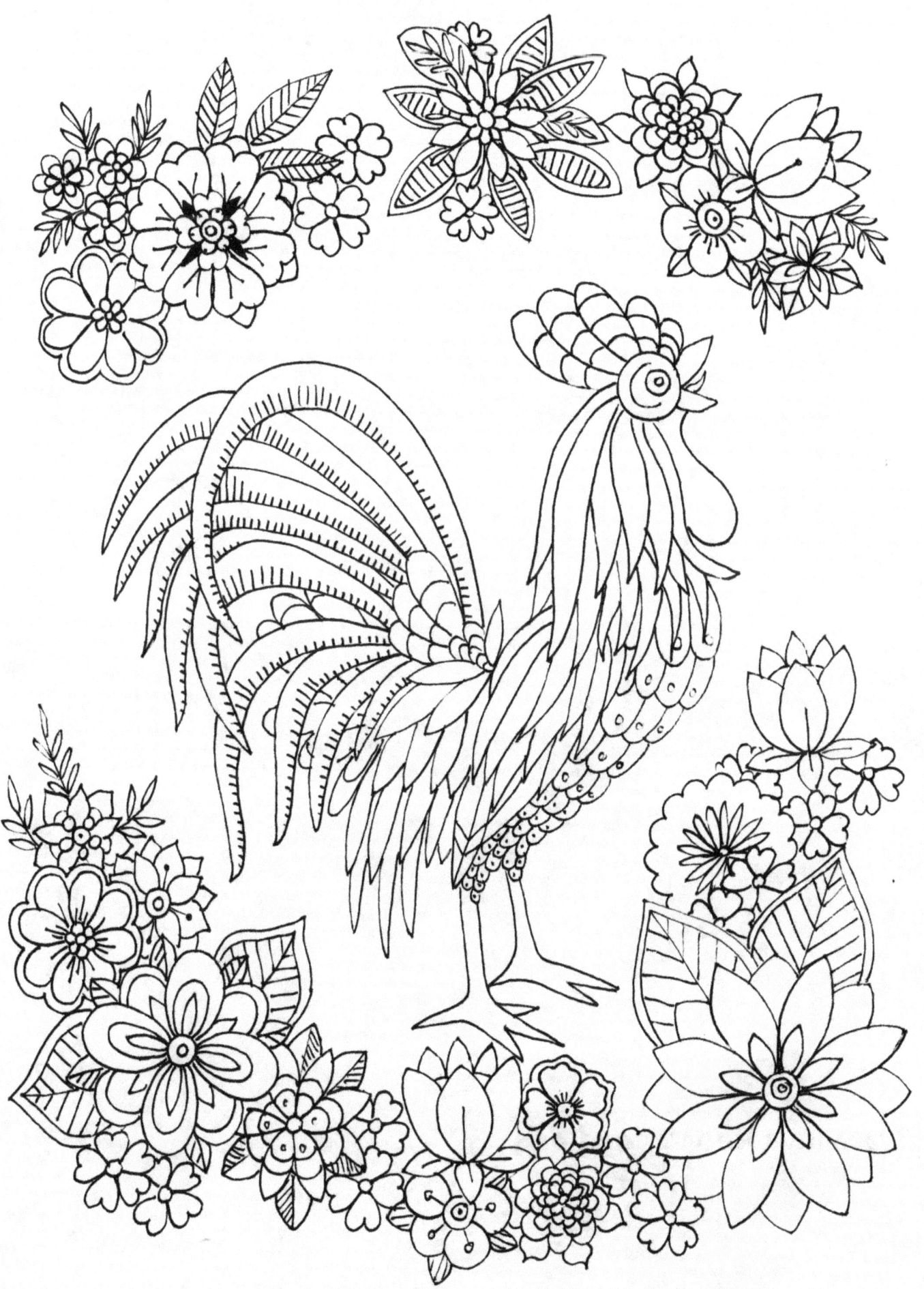

Decorative Rooster and Sun

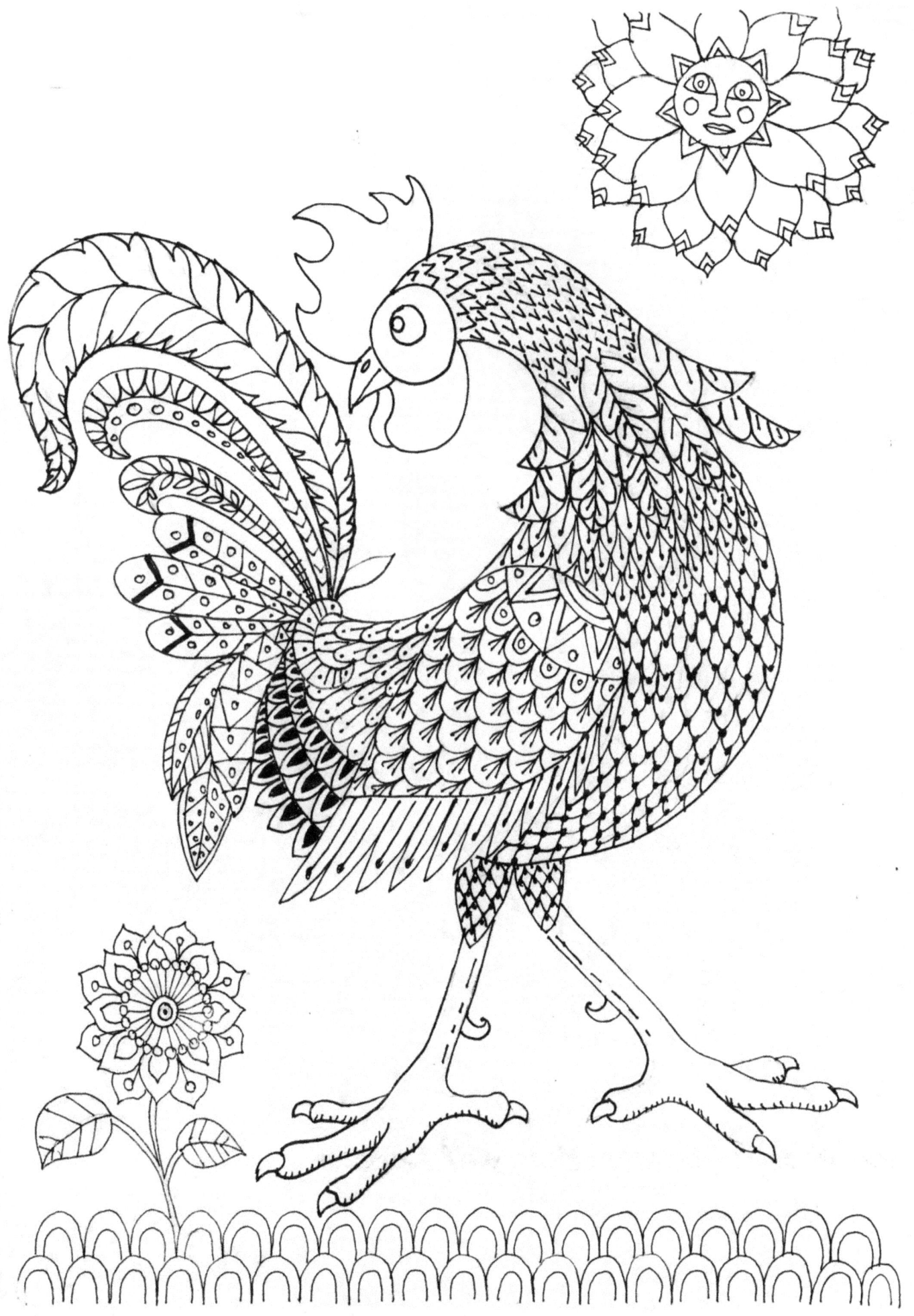

Southwestern Cowboy Boot with Rooster

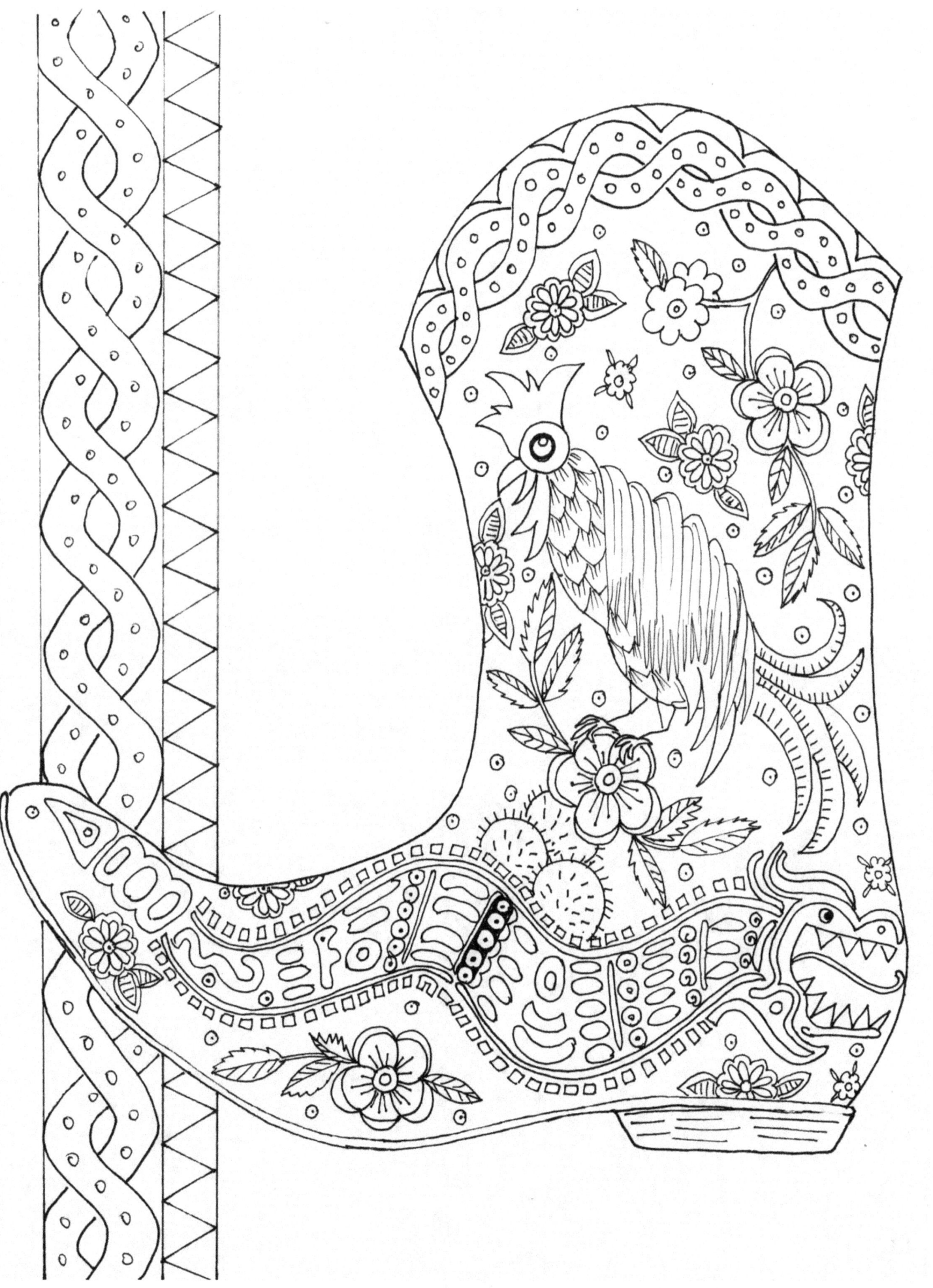

A note from the Author -

I hope you enjoyed coloring the designs in this coloring book 'Folk Art Roosters', as much as I have enjoyed creating them for you.

If you enjoyed coloring the designs in this book and don't mind sharing your opinion, please consider leaving a review on Amazon.

Thank you!

Esther Prentice

Illustrator and Author